CAREER CATALYST: 100 AI PROMPTS TO FAST-TRACK YOUR PROFESSIONAL SUCCESS

Master Intelligent Workflows, Build Your Brand, and Lead in the AI Era

TABLE OF CONTENTS

Introduction
How to Use This Book

Section 1: Career Planning and Goal Setting with AI
(Questions 1–20)

Section 2: Resume Building and Personal Branding with AI
(Questions 21–40)

Section 3: Interview Preparation and Communication with AI
(Questions 41–60)

Section 4: Upskilling, Learning, and Adaptability with AI
(Questions 61–80)

Section 5: Future Career Trends and Leadership with AI
(Questions 81–100)

Closing Reflection
About the Author

INTRODUCTION

The future of work belongs to those who can think critically, adapt quickly, and collaborate intelligently with technology.
Artificial Intelligence is no longer a distant innovation — it's a powerful tool transforming the way we plan, build, and grow our careers today.

But mastering AI is not about knowing every tool.
It's about asking the right questions — the ones that unlock smarter workflows, sharper decisions, and bold career moves.

In Career Catalyst, you'll find 100 powerful AI prompts designed to fast-track your professional success.
These questions will help you build stronger resumes, prepare for high-stakes interviews, strengthen your personal brand, learn faster, and lead confidently in an AI-driven world.

Whether you're an early professional, a career changer, an entrepreneur, or a future-focused leader, this book will guide you to use AI not just as a tool — but as a catalyst for career growth and leadership.

Success starts with asking better questions.
Let's begin.

HOW TO USE THIS BOOK

This book is designed to help you master intelligent collaboration with AI and accelerate your career growth — one powerful question at a time.

You can use it in several ways:

- **Daily Practice:** *Reflect on one prompt each day to sharpen your career planning, personal branding, or leadership skills.*

- **Focused Learning:** *Choose specific sections based on your current career goals, such as resume building, interview preparation, or future leadership development.*

- **Quick Reference:** *Open to any question whenever you need fresh ideas, strategies, or new perspectives on your professional journey.*

There are no strict rules.
This book is a tool to challenge your thinking, unlock smarter strategies, and help you lead more intentionally in an evolving career landscape.

Your next career breakthrough might just start with a single question.

SECTION 1: CAREER PLANNING AND GOAL SETTING WITH AI

(Theme: Helping readers plan, set career goals, and strategize better using AI.)

20 CAREER-BOOSTING AI PROMPTS (SECTION 1)

1. How can I use AI to map out a five-year career plan aligned with my strengths?

2. What industries should I explore based on my current skill set and emerging trends?

3. How can AI help me identify high-growth career opportunities in the next decade?

4. What new skills should I learn to future-proof my career?

5. How can I prompt AI to suggest alternative career paths based on my experience?

6. What trends should I monitor to stay ahead in my industry?

7. How can AI help me create a personalized learning roadmap for my career goals?

8. What AI-powered tools can I use to track my professional development?

9. How can I prompt AI to simulate different career scenarios and outcomes for decision-making?

10. What certifications or micro-credentials would boost my career growth fastest?

11. How can AI assist me in setting SMART (Specific, Measurable, Achievable, Relevant, Time-bound) career goals?

12. How can I analyze my career progress using AI-driven self-assessments?

13. What global job markets align with my skills, and how can AI help me research them?

14. How do I prompt AI to suggest lateral career moves that enhance my experience?

15. How can I use AI to identify the soft skills most valued in my industry today?

16. What career risks should I anticipate and how can I plan for them?

17. How can I prompt AI to help me pivot my career if my industry declines?

18. How can AI help me compare salaries, growth potential, and work-life balance across career paths?

19. What prompts can I use to get AI to suggest passion-driven career options?

20. How can I leverage AI to set short-term goals that build toward my long-term vision?

SECTION 2: RESUME BUILDING AND PERSONAL BRANDING WITH AI

(Theme: How to create powerful resumes, portfolios, and online branding using AI tools.)

20 CAREER-BOOSTING AI PROMPTS (SECTION 2)

21. How can I prompt AI to write a strong, personalized professional summary for my resume?

22. What keywords should I include in my resume for better ATS (Applicant Tracking System) optimization?

23. How can I ask AI to tailor my resume for different industries or roles?

24. How do I prompt AI to highlight my most valuable achievements clearly?

25. How can AI help me quantify my work impact with measurable results on my resume?

26. What prompts can help AI suggest alternative action verbs to make my resume more dynamic?

27. How can I prompt AI to create a one-page resume for leadership positions?

28. How do I ask AI to write customized cover letters for specific job applications?

29. How can AI assist me in creating a powerful LinkedIn headline and summary?

30. What prompts can I use to guide AI in optimizing my LinkedIn profile for recruiters?

31. How can I prompt AI to design a personal brand tagline that reflects my career goals?

32. What skills and endorsements should I highlight on my LinkedIn profile, and how can AI help suggest them?

33. How can I use AI to prepare a portfolio or website showcasing my work achievements?

34. How can I prompt AI to create an "elevator pitch" for networking events?

35. What prompts can help AI design a professional bio for conference speaking or guest articles?

36. How can I prompt AI to summarize my experience for professional award nominations?

37. What LinkedIn post ideas can AI suggest to strengthen my thought leadership?

38. How do I use AI to draft blog articles that position me as an expert in my field?

39. How can AI help me personalize outreach messages when connecting with mentors or recruiters?

40. How do I prompt AI to design a complete personal branding strategy for career advancement?

SECTION 3: INTERVIEW PREPARATION AND COMMUNICATION WITH AI

(Theme: How to use AI to prepare for interviews, improve communication, and boost confidence.)

20 CAREER-BOOSTING AI PROMPTS (SECTION 3)

41. How can I prompt AI to generate common interview questions for my target role?

42. How can AI help me craft strong, story-driven answers to behavioral interview questions?

43. What prompts can I use to practice answering tough interview questions effectively?

44. How can I ask AI to simulate a mock interview customized to my industry?

45. How can I prompt AI to suggest strong examples for answering "Tell me about yourself"?

46. What prompts can help AI generate follow-up questions I should ask interviewers?

47. How can I use AI to prepare structured responses using the STAR method (Situation, Task, Action, Result)?

48. How can I prompt AI to give feedback on my sample interview answers?

49. How do I ask AI to help me reframe weaknesses as strengths during an interview?

50. What prompts can help AI create strong questions to ask at the end of an interview?

51. How can I prompt AI to analyze job descriptions and predict likely interview topics?

52. How can AI assist me in preparing for technical or case interviews?

53. What prompts can I use to practice negotiation conversations about salary and benefits?

54. How can I ask AI to suggest strategies to manage interview anxiety and stress?

55. How can AI help me craft thank-you email templates after interviews?

56. What prompts will help AI simulate virtual interviews and provide tips for video presence?

57. How do I prompt AI to suggest communication techniques for panel interviews?

58. How can AI help me adapt my interview style for leadership or management roles?

59. How can I ask AI to generate persuasive language for presenting my unique value proposition?

60. How can AI assist in preparing for informal networking or coffee chat interviews?

SECTION 4: UPSKILLING, LEARNING, AND ADAPTABILITY WITH AI

(Theme: How to use AI to keep learning, stay flexible, and adapt to changing career demands.)

20 CAREER-BOOSTING AI PROMPTS (SECTION 4)

61. How can I prompt AI to suggest new technical skills relevant to my career path?

62. How can AI help me prioritize which certifications or courses to pursue first?

63. What prompts can help AI build a personalized learning plan based on my goals?

64. How do I use AI to research emerging skills that are in high demand?

65. How can AI help me track my progress as I build new competencies?

66. What prompts can I use to help AI identify gaps in my current skill set?

67. How can I prompt AI to recommend online learning platforms best suited to my industry?

68. How can AI help me design a daily or weekly self-learning schedule?

69. What prompts will help AI suggest books, podcasts, or videos for continuous growth?

70. How can AI assist in creating realistic timelines for achieving new career milestones?

71. How do I use AI to stay informed about changes in my industry?

72. What prompts can help AI recommend skills that align with both my interests and market needs?

73. How can AI simulate scenarios where new skills could be applied to real-world problems?

74. How do I ask AI to suggest project ideas that strengthen my portfolio while learning?

75. How can AI guide me in learning new leadership, communication, or critical thinking skills?

76. What prompts can help AI recommend cross-functional skills to diversify my career opportunities?

77. How can AI help me build resilience by preparing for disruptive changes in the workplace?

78. How do I prompt AI to suggest creative ways to practice new skills outside formal education?

79. How can AI assist me in building a growth mindset and lifelong learning habits?

80. What strategies can AI suggest to adapt quickly when facing unexpected career shifts?

SECTION 5: FUTURE CAREER TRENDS AND LEADERSHIP WITH AI

(Theme: How to anticipate future shifts, lead intelligently, and stay ahead in the AI-driven world.)

20 CAREER-BOOSTING AI PROMPTS (SECTION 5)

81. How can I prompt AI to predict major career trends over the next decade?

82. What industries are likely to grow fastest due to AI advancements, and how can AI help me explore them?

83. How can AI assist me in identifying leadership roles emerging in new industries?

84. How do I use AI to simulate challenges and opportunities in future workplaces?

85. What prompts can help AI suggest ways to build resilience against industry disruption?

86. How can AI help me design a personal innovation plan to stay competitive?

87. What prompts can guide AI to recommend ways to lead remote and hybrid teams more effectively?

88. How can AI assist me in crafting a digital-first leadership strategy?

89. How can I prompt AI to suggest ethical leadership frameworks in AI-augmented workplaces?

90. How can AI help me plan for a career that blends technology with human-centered leadership?

91. How can I prompt AI to help forecast emerging skills in leadership and management?

92. What questions should I ask AI to prepare for the global and cross-cultural impacts of AI at work?

93. How do I use AI to generate innovative solutions for sustainable leadership practices?

94. How can AI assist me in identifying and leading new entrepreneurial opportunities?

95. How can AI suggest ways to mentor the next generation of AI-literate professionals?

96. What prompts will help AI recommend thought leadership topics for future industries?

97. How can I prompt AI to help me lead organizational change driven by new technologies?

98. How can AI help me design future-proof career strategies for myself and my team?

99. How can AI assist me in maintaining emotional intelligence alongside technological expertise?

100. **How can I prompt AI to help shape a legacy of responsible innovation and leadership?**

CLOSING REFLECTION

The ability to navigate the future of work will not depend solely on knowledge — but on curiosity, adaptability, and leadership.
The questions you explored in this book are more than exercises; they are pathways to smarter thinking, bold action, and career breakthroughs.

As AI continues to transform industries and redefine success, your ability to ask better questions will set you apart.
It will help you lead, innovate, and grow in ways that technology alone cannot.

Mastering your career is not about keeping up with change — it is about shaping it.

Keep questioning. Keep learning. Keep leading.
Your next success story starts with the prompts you choose today.

ABOUT THE AUTHOR

Dr. Ruchika Jharbade is a doctor, AI researcher, and recognized young AI leader passionate about helping individuals thrive in the evolving world of intelligent work.

With a strong background in science, leadership, and future-driven innovation, she empowers professionals, entrepreneurs, and lifelong learners to build smarter careers and lead confidently in the AI era.

As a young leader in the field of artificial intelligence, Dr. Jharbade combines practical insights, strategic thinking, and a passion for lifelong learning to inspire the next generation of innovators.

Her work encourages readers to master new skills, stay adaptable, and unlock their full potential in a rapidly changing professional landscape.

When she is not writing or researching, she mentors young leaders and explores the intersections of technology, creativity, and human development.

THANK YOU FOR READING

You are now equipped with powerful questions, fresh perspectives, and intelligent strategies to lead your career forward in the AI-driven world.

Remember, true success is not about having all the answers — it's about asking the right questions at the right time.

Stay curious. Stay adaptable. Stay ahead.

Your career catalyst journey has just begun.

www.ingramcontent.com/pod-product-compliance
Lightning Source LLC
LaVergne TN
LVHW052324060326
832902LV00023B/4593